Acres of Green and Oceans of Blue: Diary of a Runaway

Poetry for the Soul

John D. Evans

Writers Club Press
San Jose New York Lincoln Shanghai

Acres of Green and Oceans of Blue: Diary of a Runaway
Poetry for the Soul

Writers Club Press
an imprint of iUniverse, Inc.

For information address:
iUniverse, Inc.
5220 S. 16th St., Suite 200
Lincoln, NE 68512
www.iuniverse.com

ISBN: 0-595-01033-4

Printed in the United States of America

This book is dedicated to my Mother, Patricia Evans. I love you more than words can ever express.

"Now faith is the substance of things hoped for, the evidence of things not seen."

Hebrews 11:1

Contents

Part Two—The Soul Speaks

Part Three—In Search of Love

Part Four—Reaching Out

Foreword

FROM THE AUTHOR

Greetings,

I am pleased to present to you, "Acres of Green and Oceans of Blue: Diary of a Runaway," my first collection of original poetry. This autobiographical book contains personal thoughts and true emotions. This book did not land in your hands by accident. There is a message waiting for you. I encourage you to take your time in reading the pages that follow, allow the words to penetrate your heart and mind, and welcome each message to embed itself deep within your soul.

My purpose in writing "Acres of Green and Oceans of Blue" is to take you on a journey of one man's life, to salute the struggles and rich heritage of Americans with African ancestry, to explore an erotic and undying quest for love, and to provide a comfort to those who may be faced with feelings of fear, loneliness, or depression. I beseech you, the reader, to aspire to achieve greatness in your life and strive to someday witness, for yourself, the lovely "Acres of Green and Oceans of Blue" of which I write.

Your Friend,

John Evans

Preface

Homage to Words

Words
They excite me
Rejuvenate me
Compel me to rise up from my bed
And write
Words
As they laugh so loudly, leap
Into my head
They orchestrate my thoughts
With harmonic symphonies
As they unite
Each newly formed subject and predicate
Dance a waltz before me
Words
They speak to me
Call out my name and
And tell me what to do
They are the Paper-mate and Mead of my mind
That dictate everything that I must jot down

In and out of the corridors of my mind
They play hide-and-go-seek
Like darling forget-me-nots

Words
They creep and crawl
into the deep crevices that they find
Becoming more and more intricate as they move along
Locating the adverbs and adjectives
Which fall into the arms of the preposition
And his many phrases
Words
They scurry about and
Run freely into the fortress of my ear
Each laugh echoed a thousand times
In the facets of my hollowness
I move to their rhythm
I dance to their beat
Words
They belong to me
And I belong to
Words

I Write

I write
Everytime I hear
That voice in my ear
I open up my mind and write
And write
I just write
Until it's right
With all my might
I don't fight
I just write
I must write
I have to write
And write
And write
And write

I write when
Thoughts begin
To control my mental pen,
I relax, release,
Then
I write
I just write

Until it's right

With all my might

I don't fight

I just write

I must write

I have to write

And write

And write

And write

I dance to her music

To her song, I sing along

Uncontrollably, Can't stop

The voice I hear lingers on

I close my eyes to sleep

Then all night,

I write

Until it's right

With all my might

I don't fight

I just write

I must write

I have to write

And write

And write

And write

In the morning
Afternoon
Or middle of the night,
My passion
My true love
My desire is to write

Acknowledgements

Thank you, Lord, for empowering me with the strength and determination needed to complete this work. For without your love and grace, I am nothing.

To my Mother, Patricia Evans; sisters, Rita and Tricia; best friend, Terrance; and high school sweetheart, DeLondra, this one's for you! For being constant sources of inspiration for me, I give my love and appreciation. May God's mercy and blessings continue to shower upon you.

To all of my teachers, especially Mrs. Downs and Mrs. Hegarty of John M. Smyth Elementary School, thank you. To my church families, Greater Rock M. B. Church (Chicago, Illinois), Mount Moriah M. B. Church (Atlanta, Georgia) and Second Ebenezer M. B. Church (Detroit, Michigan), thank you for being such a great part of my life. To the National Association for the Advancement of Colored People (NAACP), thank you for sponsoring the annual ACT-SO Competition, which inspired me to hold fast to my dreams. To my countless supporters, thank you for believing in me.

To every man, woman, boy and girl that has ever passed my way and inspired me to write – many thanks to each and every one of you.

Part One

Enter My World

My Song

On one fateful day
In seventy four, April third
I received the gift of life
And my song was heard
There I lay, so small, so still
With my mom alone
She whispered, "hello,"
To her son
And a world unknown
With long, curly hair and
A voice that would ring
A child who never saw his dad
Sure had a song to sing
So sweet, so pure, so innocent
Verse one, I did begin

My cry was loud and grip was strong
Wrapped in choc'late skin
Come into my world,
Sense the hope, feel despair
In a cold and lonely place
With gangs everywhere
Men cursed, played the blues,
And pushed me to the side
From the noise and the smoke
Poor baby could not hide

I now dread the lullaby
Of cradles in a tree
Because, in time, my sisters came
We went from four to three
A sister that I hardly knew
Was victim of a crime
Because the thug was just a lad

For it, he did no time

To hide from bullies and the thugs
We stayed inside our room
All day long we played alone,
But couldn't escape the gloom
Skinny, frail with braided hair
I looked just like a girl
When tears flooded my face at night
In mom's arm, I would curl
When gangs came, crowded around,
I didn't know what to do
I then found refuge in church
And shouted my verse two
My aunt and cousins lived up high
Never far away
When food was scarce and cupboards bare,
With them we all would stay
Full of hope, yet full of pain,

My heart beat with a fire
To feel loved, to be free
Was my strong desire

Freedom from a world of fear
Is what I had to hold
To be strong, to be tall,
Admired, fierce and bold
"Amazing Grace" and "Precious Lord"
Flowed freely from my soul
I yearned for a guiding light
And place to be made whole
When I rose to sing,
Others hushed to hear my song
I chose to leave the hood one-day
And took my dreams along
My mom and friends were by my side
But didn't want me to go

I pressed my way on to the South
A place I did not know
There I earned my first degree
To prove it could be done
I learned later that in life,
We all, someday, will run

A smoke, a drink, a club or two
I thought could do no harm
But on one, eerie night,
Music grabbed my arm,
Pulled me to the dance floor,
We swayed to the beat
We danced up close and in no time,
Felt our bodies heat
When we kissed, I knew within
That this life was mine
I had to live and be free
True love, I had to find

From heart to heart, I searched for love
The source of my verse three
Through tear-stained eyes, looking back
At bitter memories
It was a day
A fateful day
In seventy four, April third
And just like then,
On today,
My song must be heard,

My song must be heard,

My song must be heard

Life in A Dungeon

Winner of the 1992 NAACP ACT-SO Award

It is dark.
Tears flood my face.
In this, a chamber of solitude,
    I
    kneel
    quietly.

The fears I have,
Overpower my pains.
Sensations of loneliness
Shorten my every breath
As the sounds of
          Stomping feet,
       Slamming doors,
     And my beating heart
Cause me to quiver.

I am able to smell my last meal
Because the memory still lingers.
The omnipotent aroma of despair
Fills the air I breathe,
As the
    Drip-drops
Of nasty waters
Bring chills to my shivering soul.

I am hushed
By my hunger for freedom
And lulled
into meditation
                by dreams,
my dreams,
Prisoners,
In the fortress of my mind.

This is my life
And my plea.

A life in a lonesome place,
                    Cold,
            Dark,
        And secluded
Tortured,
By the hands of fear and pain
Alone,
In search for light
I call it a dungeon.

The Pot

Life
is but a crock-pot of
a whole bunch of stuff
thrown together,
all mixed up,
tossed
A medley of precious things,
carefully selected,
delicately hand-picked
from Mother Earth,
perfectly seasoned,
placed over a flame,
then stirred
slowly
by huge,
loving hands

Genesis

Bursting like a river
Of sweet coconut cream
Rushing down, uniting with
A gentle, flowing stream
Of lazy lakes and soothing seas
Of waters, warm and blue
Dancing with a steady beat
Like drops of morning dew
Landing safely on a seed
That will never close
But open to someday become
The arms of a rose

One Special Day

Today is a special day

One full of bliss

For on this day

God opened my eyes

With a gentle kiss

A day when the breath of life

Was immersed into my soul

When love and mercy

Joined at once

Just to make me whole

A special day it was

When my first cry was heard

The day when God came to me

And softly spoke the word

"Wake up child,

Open your eyes

Let me see your face"

He then shined his light

From Heaven above and

Showered me with his grace

With heavenly soil in his hands,

He molded me, his child

Offered me his precious love

I answered with a smile

From the elements of life

So uniquely made

Into the arms of a soul,

Most gently laid

I am here and I am blessed

In an awesome way

The day that God gave life to me

Was one special day

In the Sky

Twisting

Twirling

Spinning

Flowing gently in the wind

Flying

Soaring

Running

So high

Wild

So free

Going round and round

Lost in time

Circles of life

Circles in life

Just twisting

And twirling

Flying and

Soaring

A ribbon

A long, dark

Shiny

Ribbon

When I Stand

When I stand
All eyes
They stick, like glue, to me
They fix onto my every move
My legs are all you see

I captivate the mind
With my stature, tall and lean
When passing by, you stop and stare
A giant you have seen

When I stand
Your head
Will turn and take a twist
When I move from place to place
My presence, you can't miss

A walking monument

That hovers above man

With a height that you can't touch

I tower

When I stand

Wake-up Call

They stand

Perched

Outside my window

Watching me

Laughing

Talking about me

At my lying down to sleep

My kinky locks

My round nose

At my high cheek bones

They laugh

At my long feet

They laugh

At my long legs

They laugh

At the very noises I make

They laugh

And laugh and

Laugh

All night long

Perched

Outside my window

Watching me

Talking about me

Laughing

The Runaway

With long, aching feet

I run

To the thump,

The thump

Of a lonely heart

It burns with a fire

That will never die

Haunted by my very soul

Shouting aloud my name

From dusk to dawn

I run

Searching wildly for myself

For an answer that has no breath

Where love has no sight

And hope holds me tight

Without arms

Blindly sprinting along

A path called life,

One continuous, constant maze

That twists and turns

And makes me weak

As I run

Into huge, broken walls

Like a Man

Like a newborn babe
I cry
I weep and sob and moan
I stomp my feet
Refuse to eat
Can not be left
alone

Like a tower
I stand
Monumental
Gift of grace
My smile so wide
And walk of pride
Cause hope to wash
My face

Like a budding rose

I bloom

Despite the winds that blow

A work of art

Bestills the heart

A gift with love

To show

Like a hummingbird

I sing

Melodious

Songs of praise

I see my prize

Up in the skies

Great Giver

Of my days

Like a lion

I roar

So loud, so fierce, so deep

Strong and brave

Son of a slave

Faith, I too,

shall keep

Like a gem

I shine

A treasure, tattered, tossed

New, yet old

Rich past, I'm told

No longer

Am I lost

Like a stallion

I leap

Over mountains, 'round each hill

Drenched with rain

And soaked in pain

Relief I long

To feel

Like an eagle

I soar

Above the sea and land

Swift and bold

My fate, I hold

In my heart

and hand

Like a soldier

I am

Destined to be me

In my plight

I will fight

'til victory I see

I AM A MAN

I dream

A burning fire's in my eye

Born of Kings

My voice will ring

Until the day

I die

Part Two

The Soul Speaks

Speaking of the Storm

You contemptuous creature
To slight my wrath with your sedation,
To entertain me with window dressing,
To turn your back toward my wind
And blanket your ears from my bellow,
Sensing my ever presence,
All night, you cuddle and hold yourself
While sinking deeper and deeper
Into a haze of incoherence
Your pseudo-soft pillow of satisfaction
Barely holds up your weary head
With contentment chanting a lullaby,
You dream a dismal dream
But how can you slumber
In the midst of my thunder,

My band of bongos that beat

In the sky?

How can you have rest

In the midst of my rain

That falls in drops and runs a race

Landing and dancing a jig

Atop your rickety rooftop?

In the midst of my storm

With winds that rock your cradle

And pound against your pane

That cause your shutters to shake

And walls to break?

My force is your frailty,

My strength, your shortcoming

I am the quaking of the Earth

I am the rumbling of the seas

I am the dusty shadow of the air

I am the wind that lifts each wing

I am the rushing of each cloud

The scurry of beings that

Trample on tumultuous terrain

Wake up heathen

Most defiant one

Open your eyes—watch me work

Lend me your ear—hear my voice

I am the storm

Hear me as I speak

Beat of the Drum

Muzzle the mouth

Chain each foot

Lift and

Carry

Away

Treasures, gone

Kindred, gone

And darkness in the day

Moans into the black of night

Shivering

Cold and

Still

Crying

Alone and

Aching with

Wounds that will not heal

Terrified and hungry

Toiling,

Naked

Sore and

Weak

Forced to keep silent

Can not live

Breathe

Or speak
Rotting in filthy rags

Forced to suffer

Sweat

To bleed

Suffocating, dying

Strangled by the stench of greed

Looking up, crying out

Reaching for the sun

Close your eyes

Feel my breeze

Hear

The beating drum

Born of Men

I am a son of the greatest

That ever was,

That ever will be

Born of men

Who rose like the sun

When light, they could not see

The son of survivors

That wore

The shackles,

Felt the shame

Across the oceans and the seas

Ruthless predators came

The son of leaders

Mighty

Kings and Queens adorned

Of their precious gems,

Stripped

Naked, tossed and torn

The son of servants

Humble

Spirited, tried and true

They called for help and

Cried for peace

Like only they could do

The son of warriors

I am

Prepared for a fight

Ready to speak my mind

And truth, I'll find

With chains, no longer in sight

I am a son of the greatest

That ever was,

That ever will be

Born of men who rose

Like the sun

When light they could not see

Voice in the Night

With an eerie, lingering voice

It beckons me

By my name, it summons me

With constant, lasting ringing

Each high-pitched shrill anticipates the next

A never-ending round of

Dark, dissonant chords

That echo into the night

Mysteriously hovering over my head,

Bouncing off naked walls,

Filling the openness of my huge ears,

Like a phantom

Crying into the night

Long, desperate cries

Left unanswered

From the Soul of John

A man is what I am

Though I wear

A ball and chain

I long to feel the sun

But am showered

By the rain

Bound and gagged by injustice

I fight to live and speak

My voice

Criticized—cast to the side

Sold without a choice

In this race with time
From thieves of life, I flee
Blinded by the masks they wear
And those who linger to see

Though bruised and broken,
I shout
Out of my bleeding heart,
I cry
Left alone,
Through fields I roam
Tortured, then left to die

Stripped,
In empty fields I dream
Naked
No place to go
In a land, my sweat has built
My home,
I long to know

Not even a glimmer of hope
Can I see through my
Blood-shot eyes
I won't give up or turn back now
But look toward the skies

In a land so drunk with sin
I speak a sober mind
Loose and free
How can I be?
When staggering from behind

A stranger in this dreary place
With pride, I shall stand
Strong and tall,
Firm, broad and all
In this, a foreign land

An innocent child I'll bring
Into this way of life, unfair

Abused

For having skin so dark

Adorned

With silky, black hair

My dreams, old and stale

Suffocated

By the stench of greed

I'm weary of slaving my life away

To fill another's need

I, too, am a man

Hymns I sing—drums I play

From my soul,

I dance in a

Riveting, rhythmic way

I want to know my name

In this life that's like a game

The rules for Tom

And me, Tom's John

Will never be the same

John Doe Speaks

Hey!

Ya' gotta' minute?
My name is John Doe
With no home,
Through these streets I roam
I have no place to go

Without a blanket for my head
I'm drownin' in the rain
Flooded by tears
Been livin' for years
In poverty and pain

Each new day is old
As each one before

I sleep in slums

And live on crumbs

Cold, desp'rate, sore

Please

Don't walk away!

I need a helpin' han'

I've grown weak,

Can't hardly speak,

Walk, or even stan'

I know that when I'm near

My stench is all you smell

My wraps all tattered

All broken and battered

Everything around me's stale!

I can use some help

Folk like you, keep passin' by

You push and shove
As I beg, out of
A bleedin' heart an' cry

Don't turn away this time
You gotta' see that I'm in need
'Causa this storm
I need to feel warm,
Protected, yeah, and free

Though empty, my days are full
With the darkness of the night
I am the one
Friends, I have none
I see no hope in sight

A stranga' in this worl'
I breathe, but do not live
You laugh and play

Enjoy the day

But have no time to give

I'm sorry if I'm a botha'

But I look to you for hope

I can't have rest

Until I'm blessed

With this pain, I can not cope

Cain't you help me this one time

And not spit at my face,

Push me to the side,

While tryin' to hide

My presence in this place?

All right!

All right!

Go on!

If you must, just go!

Why diss the man

With the outstretched han'

The man you call John Doe

Black Boy

Hey Black boy!
Get outta' here
You need to go back home
You're ugly, loud
And dirty while
Down my street
You roam

You lurk around
All day and night,
Which proves to me
You're rude
You drink my wine,
Want things of mine
Devour all' my food

Hey Black boy!

Don't stop here

My threats,

They are real

Just try

To come back here again

My whip,

Your back will feel

I'm tired of your

Shuffle-along

With freedom in this land

You moan and cry

And beg out of a

Filthy, greedy hand

I'm in control of things

And this,

Boy, you know

I'm destined to

Remind your kind

Everywhere you go

Hey Black boy!

Get on

I don't want to see your face

A disgrace to man

I have a plan

To rid you of this place

Stand up

Look around

Cain't you see Black boy?

My neighborhood

And way of life

Your presence will destroy

No matter what it takes

I'm bound to run you away

You are just a passerby,

But me?

I'm here to stay

The Answer

You can ask,
"Why are you mad?"
The answer
You should know
You remind me of
Your foolish ways
Everywhere I go

To the North and
Then the South
You are always there
Hating me from
My toes
To my curly hair

From my stylish
Manner of dress
When I walk, I glide
With my resonating voice,
I speak my mind
With pride

You insult me
To my face
But try to coat it
With a smile
You extend to me
Your dirty hand
Despise'n me
All the while

When you speak
I'm not your boy

And you, the only man
When my mouth
Proclaims a word,
On that word, I stand

When I'm down
And feeling low
You, inside, are glad
This fight is old
Just dragging on
That's why I am so mad

The Man I Met

I met Envy

He was slick

A mask covered his face

He studied my moves

Just hated my groove

Wanted me out of the place

I shook his hand

He was weak

Afraid and insecure

Pierced me with blue

Didn't flinch, I knew

His pressures I could endure

I smelled his breath

It was tart

Hate flowed from his lips
When I stepped out of line
By being so fine
He lashed me with his whip

The taste of pow'r
Propelled him so
So hungry, I was his meat
My zeal, did he savor
My spicy, bold flavor
But gave him no time to eat

I played his game
Just like a champ
Though each round he seemed to win
When he swung and I blocked
Everyone shouted, was shocked
"How could he challenge the man?"

I heard his voice

'Twas in the dark

In front, on sides and behind

I could not conform

Refused to transform

An exit, I had to find

I felt his rage

It was clear

He hated my curly hair

Couldn't stand my stride

Slow me down, he tried

Into my eyes, couldn't stare

I was his foe

Thought I was damned

For I was on my own

No one said a word

To save this caged bird

Mistreated, then left alone

Why I Call In

Aaaah…

The birds are singing
Church bells ringing
Look at the flowers bloom

Alarms are soundin'
My heart's poundin'
Darkness fills my room!

I roll out of bed
Oh God! I'm dead!
I smack the clock
Slept like a rock
I want to cry

And sob and sigh

Five minutes, please?

I scratch and sneeze

All right! All right!

Turn on the light

I'm up, yet down

Can't smile, but frown

I whine

I pout

I drag my feet

I'm starved,

But have no time to eat

No shower can open

Up these eyes

Nor suds that drown my hair

I'm wet and cold

Feeling tired and old

My face gives me a scare

Tick

Tock

I rush, I run

Tick

Tock

I scream

Tick, tock

No fair, no fun

Just like a

Terrible dream

To primp and prime

I have no time

Where's my shoe

What should I do?

Nothing to wear

No time to spare

Oh, just great!

A sock, no mate

Traffic, my foe
Out there, can't go
My boss, unkind
And keys?
Can't find
The world's a cloud
I shout aloud,
"Give back my sleep
This time, I keep"

Where's my bed
On this morn' I dread?
Save me from this doom!

Aaaah…

The birds are singing
Church bells ringing
Look at the flowers bloom

The Invitation

Get on the bus Black Man!
Don't get left behind
Don't hesitate
The bus awaits
Get on board and ride

Sit up front and ride
Sit up tall and ride
Hold your head up high and ride
Ride!
Black Man!
Ride!

Speak your voice and ride
Live your dream and ride
Wipe the tearstain from your eye

And ride!

Black Man!

Ride!

Your heart beats with a fire

Ride!

The ticket is in your hand

Ride!

Listen to your soul—it cries

Ride!

Black Man!

Ride!

Get on the bus Black Man!

Don't get left behind

Don't hesitate

The bus awaits

So ride, Black Man, ride

Ride!

Black Man!

Ride!

The Seed

It's all in the seed
What's the seed?
Your smile's the seed
Your shake and
Your charm

You are the seed
What is the seed?
Your dream's the seed
Your goal and
Your drive

You have the seed
You own the seed
It's all in the seed

It's in the seed

So plant the seed

Water it

Nurture it

Control the fate

Of the seed

It's all in the seed

The Seed

Watch it bud

Watch it blossom

Watch it bloom

You have the seed

You own the seed

It's all in the seed

The seed

Rich seed

Delicate mustard seed

Grab hold of the seed

Speak to the seed

Believe in the seed

At dawn, a seed

At dusk, a seed

Tomorrow's Great Oak

You have the seed

You own the seed

You are the seed

I Am

I am the sweet, delicate morsel

Rolling gently on sensitive buds

The intoxicating stream of ideas

That falls fresh,

So pure and free

I am the soft, soothing sound

That lulls nature to sleep

And alarm of life,

Calling out

Rise and behold my pleasantries!

They surround you,

Fill you,

Engulf you,

Move you,

Shake you,

Sing to your soul

My incantations are your music

I am a poet

Because I dream poetic phrases

In my sleep

I am on fire

Ignited by its power

I am, too, a poem

Part Three

In Search of Love

The Web

Let me catch you

In the web

Of my arms

Let me guide you

Lead you

Into the heart of my soul

The soul of my heart

Moved by motions

Of a smooth groove

Charged up

Tangled up,

Wrapped up

Interwoven

Locked

Apart, yet one

Reaching and holding on

Hoping and grabbing

for love,

my love,

caught

in the web

Tell Me Why

You ask me, why?

I'll tell you why

It's because you see me everyday

And roll your eyes at me,

Cut your eyes at me

Then quickly turn away

When you know that I'm near

You move away

Why?

Have I wronged you?

Have I insulted you in any way?

You don't even know my name

I know that when you sleep at night

You fight off dreams of me

When I catch a glimpse of your eye

I feel the yearning

Yet, you allow me to slip away

From your grasp, from your grip

Day after day, after

Day after day

Why?

You fight the feelings

You torture yourself

You treat me this way

Yet, you ask me,

Why?

Why don't you tell me

Why

Lost at Sea

Drifting aimlessly along

A cold, motionless stream

So dark, so empty, so still

Void of life

No flicker of light

Seeping of air

Or change of seasons

Lost

Slowly sinking into

A bottomless pit of tears

Landing deep within the soul

Just lingering on

Drifting along

Living

Without love

To Love a Man

To admire a loving father
With his firm, yet gentle hand
To revere a savior, risen
Is to love a man

To play all day with brother
To laugh and joke with friend
To enjoy the presence of uncle
Is to really love a man

To learn from a teacher
Or cheer an athlete, his fan
To close your eyes and pray at night
Is to love a man

To know that you are safe
Warmed by his touch and
Feel comfort when you know he's near
Is to love a man

To honor a loving father
With his firm, yet gentle hand
To love another being
Is to also love a man

Mine

Where is my poet?
With his lovely, lyrics, long
Or that jazz musician
Playin' my fav'rite song
Where is my boxer?
Givin' out his black and blues
Or that man behind the bar
Moving me with booze
Where is my doctor?
Somewhere really getting' paid
Or my ruff-neck brotha'
Sportin' Tims and a fade
Where is my quarterback?
Holding me so strong
Or my point guard

Standing tall on feet so long
Where is my weed-head?
Puffin', blowin', makin' me high
Or my corp'rate exec?
In his dry-cleaned shirt and tie
Where is my lawyer?
Just waitin' to plead my case
Or my milk chocolate cadet
With his handsome face
Where is my teacher?
Going through his text
Or no limit soldier
Askin' me, "Who is next?"
Where is my track star?
Runnin', 'round a track
Or hard-bodied ex-con
Never looking back

Where is my student?

All buried in his books

Or my supermodel

With his sexy, savvy looks

Where is my personal chef?

Prepared to wine and dine

Where is he?

That special man

That man I shall call

MINE

Mirage

There he is
The man of my dreams
A wanted man
A real man
Confident, dark and strong
A fine, choc'late morsel
Poured by the hands of God
Into a perfect, human sculpture
The soft, velvet shirt he wears
Hugs his chiseled arms
They captivate me
Cause me to sweat and yearn for him
I am weak
My eyes wander
Downward

Toward his bulging thighs

That burst in every angle

Of his tightly fitted, black jeans

Warmed by his natural body heat

I ache

To release from his heavy boots

Frightfully long, flawless feet

His head, so shiny, bald and brown

Is a round Hershey's Kiss

His smile calls me by name

My response?

One long, hard gulp

The ice makes music against my sweaty glass

I am seduced

By his dark, brown eyes

His seductive, dark brown eyes

They welcome me to come closer

I am captivated by his sensuous smile

His eyes are locked into mine

He's coming!

He's coming this way!

My heart races faster with each long stride that he makes

Salty waters begin to shower my face and body

My entire desperate body

Damn!

My hands—they tremble at every thought

Of him touching me, holding me, feeling me

In all the right places,

Touching me, holding me, feeling me

With all of his manhood,

Touching me, holding me, feeling me

Belonging only to me

For as long as I want him to be

For as long as I can stand it

He is coming closer,

Closer,

Closer,

Look at him

An awesome creature

The man of my dreams

The Big Secret

What's up man?
With that big, wide smile
I am entranced
By the glow in your eyes
What's up with that?
Your laughter lighting up
This dim, dry space
Cooling it, moisturizing it
Onto your every word,
I hang
Why is it?
That you lie to me
Tell stories to me and
Smile at me
Without really talking to me

Allowing me to hear

The soothing sounds

That you really want,

In your heart,

To share

How is it?

That you do what you do

That you feel what you feel,

On the inside,

Keeping captive your true self,

Your true emotions

Stop lying to me

Tell me what's on your mind

Let me feel you

Let me know you

Let me go with you

To that special place

That you've been to,

In your wildest dream,

Wishing I, too, were there

What's up with all of that?

I've watched your walk

That cool and gentle stride

That smooth and graceful glide

I've listened to you talk

That deep hypnotizing voice

I've touched your hand

Immersed with a heat,

It soothed my body, sore

I can hear the moaning

of your soul and

The beat—beat of your heart

Your body aches

Just like mine

It is weak

It yearns

For a love, a sweet love

A passionate, real love

A wild, erotic adventure

One that I, only I, can give

That's all right man

Don't tell me

Don't say a word

I know

I know how you feel

I know what you want

When you light up like a candle

When you know I'm near

When you make me laugh

Like everything is just fine

When you shake my hand

With a tight and groping grip

I know you

I feel you

So don't say a word

Don't tell me a thing

Just keep on doing

Those things that you do

Those masculine, sexy

Things that you do

It's all right

Don't tell me

Don't say a word

'Cause I know

Man, I know

The Star

I lay awake all through the night
Peeping out of my window
Hoping you'd stop by
When someone approaches,
All I can do is cry
Because you are the star of my life

I toss and turn all night in my bed
Wishing you were here with me
And when the phone rings
I rush to answer
This love is such a crazy thing
Because you are the star of my life

I need you in my life
I love the twinkle in your eye

It feels me with a love

That I can't deny

All I need is you

Because you are the star of my life

I want to have you

Hold you in my arms forever

I'll never let you go away

But keep you by my side

Because you are the star of my life

You are the star of my life

Sweet Love

To gaze into your lovely, brown eyes
Or feel your silky, smooth skin
To hold you close in my arms
And feel your love within
To rub your long, hard back
And run my fingers through your hair
To kiss, softly, your precious lips
While into your eyes, I stare
To dance all night, on time, up close
Caressing you, so dear
Whispering softly words of love
Most gently, into your ear
To watch, with you, the setting sun
Then glistening, morning dew

To hold you in my arms is

To make sweet love to you

The Bomb

Sex is the bomb

That each man, someday,

Desires to explore,

To investigate, to study

To feel for himself

In perfect time,

Up close, and personally

With rhythmic motions

On a syncopated beat

Going in and out

Fast then slow

'Round and 'round

Around each curve and

Around each bend

He, too, a lethal weapon,

Enters each open space

Carefully poking about,

Taking care

Of the precious commodity

That is his

One that is essential

To the ongoing circle of life

Always ready to explode,

To ignite,

To become one with him

This is the bomb and

The bomb is sex

When I Think of You

As I gaze into the sky
And adore a sparrow in flight
Or lie down near a stream
Warmed by the sun's radiant light
When I listen to the harmonies
Of God's creatures singing their song
I think only of you
Oh for your presence, I do long

As I stroll through open fields
And breathe in its simple perfume
Or pause to praise a precious wonder
From the flowery beds that bloom
When I think of clouds, so soft
Or the majestic seas, so blue

When I am soothed by a gentle breeze
I think only of you

As I watch the butterflies play
Flying with fervor, flying free
Or run my fingers through sand
Under the shade of a palm tree
When I smile with a grateful sigh
Or am bestilled by my peace within
I wish, each time, that you were near
My heart, you did mend

As I think to myself
And search within my soul
I capture sentiments of you
Your affection has made me whole
When I close my eyes and see your face
I know these feelings are true
When I think of beauty
That is when I think of you

First Sight

Love found me when
I first beheld
Your lovely face
My smile could not hide
The joy inside
Enchanted by your grace

Love found me when
I was lost
In your eyes
Where have you been?
My charming friend
Heaven beneath the skies

Love found me when
I shared with you a dance

That night we met
Hugged, kissed and sweat
'Twas fate and not mere chance

Love found me when
You took my hand and led the way
Though strong, I was weak
And proud, yet meek
I wanted you to stay

Love found me when
Your touch soothed my body, sore
Your gentle hand
Warm, loving man
Made me want you more

Love found me when
Together we did dream

Under the tree
You and me
Near a flowing stream

Love found me when
I inhaled the juices of your hair
With a joy that is real
And affection we feel
This love we're meant to share

Love found me when
I could not let you go
More than a friend
My heart, you did win
In love, we both will grow

An Aries Thing

I guess it's an Aries thing
To feel the way I do
To love someone
In such short time and
Know the love is true

It must be an Aries thing
Love is
A part of me
Sweet sentiments, I must hear
And lover, I must be

An Aries will spark
The flames
Of a fireplace

And fall in love
With the single touch
Of a warm embrace

From the heart, an Aries
Will write
And out of the soul, we sing
But to do it all
For a thing called LOVE
Must be an Aries thing

Waiting

Where are you?
"Call back," you said,
"Later," but
you're not there

What should I do?
Wait, wipe my eyes
While at the phone
I stare?

This time apart
Helped me to know
How much
I feel for you

When we first met
I knew within
What your charm
Could do

Where are you?
Your soft, sweet smile,
Your laugh
And handsome face

What should I do?
I miss your
Touch, the
Warmth of your embrace

Why must I wait?
On you to call
When you
Should be with me

Is this my fate?

Waiting, my friend,

Wondering

Where you could be?

Through the Night

I know how it feels to be lonely
All alone, in the dark, by myself
But I know that the sun will shine again
If I could make it through the night

There's no need to feel discouraged
Suffering, alone, in so much pain
Wishing you were right by my side
As I make it through the night

The stars portray a picture of you
And the wind, it whistles your name
The moon makes me want you more
And your love throughout the night

I know how it feels to be lonely

All alone, in the dark, by myself

But I know that the sun will shine again

Once I've made it through the night

Yes

Am I the one you're looking for?

With lovely, dark brown eyes

Am I the one you're reaching for?

Across the land and sky

Am I the one you're searching for?

With a heart of gold

Am I the one you're longing for?

And a love untold

Am I the one you're praying for?

Looking to the hills

Am I the one you're living for?

And joy I may reveal

Am I the one you're hoping for?

A never-ending quest

Am I the one you're looking for?

The answer, I hope, is yes

Part Four

Reaching Out

True Desire

what is your true desire?/ that I love no more?/ that I dream no more?/ that I no longer am free?/ that I do no more?/ that I say no more?/ that I no longer be me?/ should I blanket my heart with pain and muffle my mouth in fear?/ mask who I really am as if I were not here?/ is it your desire for me to dry up, crumble, burn?/ to lower my head in shame like my life took a bad turn?/ be blown away by your prejudicial wind?/ to cry alone while harsh words you send?/ what is your true desire?/ that I love no more?/ that I dream no more?/ that I no longer am free?/ that I do no more?/ that I say no more?/ that I no longer be me?

Alone

alone

in this cold, dark place

so quiet, so still

pondering

on life

asking, why?

afraid

and lonely

why?

searching

deep within my soul

my yearning, crying soul

for answers

unable to move

unable to live

unable to love

to feel love

alone

here

in this empty place

reaching out

to the nothingness

that surrounds me

feeling

all

alone

A Letter from Ms. Understood

Dear Judgemental One:

I am Ms. Understood
Because I love what I love
And you don't feel I should
I love from the pit of my heart
And that love is returned to me
I'm not here to cause you harm
And this, you do not see

You mistreat me day by day
Though I, too, have dreams
You feel that I'm a fallen star

But things aren't like they seem

I do dream—from my soul

And, yes, my dreams come true

You can not judge me when

My soul came not from you

You scandalize my name

Because you dislike where I go

You can't hate a place

That you don't even know

I was also born free

With a life that I love

I am here and I am blessed

With gifts from above

You call me a freak

Because of things you feel I've done

But I now overlook defame,

Live and press on
I inspire others to smile
To speak, with pride, their voice
How I carry on in life
Is my own choice

You say that I've transgressed
Because I feel the way I feel
On the inside, is a heart
With feelings that are real
I am very special
In life, free to be me
For you to mock and call me names
Is such a travesty

I love life and who I am
Regardless of what you say
I must live and be me
Each and every day

I am an individual
To try'n be you isn't good
Until I'm gone,
I'll be myself

Sincerely,

Ms. Understood

The Fight

It is so cold out here

So bitter cold

My trembling body aches

Covered with frost

A hungry, hovering frost

Constantly biting

My fingers,

My toes,

My nose

All frozen

I'm stuck

Can not move

My eyes are fixated

By the cold waters

That have stained them

My breath is so real

I can see it

Each exhale

Is a sign of the relief

That I long to feel

It is so cold out here

So bitter cold

The winds

That cause me to shake

Are fierce

My arms are numb

My legs are numb

I'm about to break

Into pieces

Many small pieces

As I wrestle

Temptations

To surrender

I stand still

Just

Stand

Still

Sometimes

Sometimes I feel
like a baby bird
swiftly falling from the sky
Toward the ground
For Earth, I'm bound
No time left to fly

Sometimes I feel
I'm in a dream
Or a world, unreal
Suffering, in time,
will no longer be mine
and pain, no longer feel

Sometimes I feel
like a sinking ship

Knowing I may die
Holding the hand
of my best friend
as we, together, cry

Sometimes I feel
like I've lost a race
before it has even begun
Cut short my lead,
Reduced my speed
The race I could have won

Sometimes I feel
like a beggar in need
of a nickel or dime
My esteem, low
With nowhere to go
But only
some of the time

Song for Charlie

Dear Ol' Charlie Brown
I wonder where you have gone
You've packed up all your things
Now I'm all-alone

Dear Ol' Charlie Brown
You didn't tell me where you'd be
So busy running away
You didn't have time for me

Thoughts of you, my friend
Dance throughout the day
Even in the late night hour
I hear things that you would say

Your sense of humor

And loads of wit

Where could they have gone?

I can't help but wonder

If I somehow made you run

I wish that we could talk ol' pal

And find out

What went wrong?

Why did you leave

Without looking back

Leaving me this sad song

Curtain Call

How long will this
Life of mine last
A year, month,
Day or two?

When the last page
Of my life
is read,
What will I then do?

Feel weary and weak
From life's sojourn
And ready
For my sleep?

Giving away my
Treasures and all
For nothing,
I may keep

Will I become
A stranger of life
From me,
Will all men flee?

When God's great sun
Bids me farewell
I wonder where I'll be

Behind the walls
Of a place
In Peace
Calm and still

Or absorb

such sounds as

Help me!

Oh Lord!

Ease this pain I feel!

Will I need a friend,

Feeling alone

Will there be

Someone there

Loving me,

Holding my hand,

Someone who

Really cares

When my sight begins

To fade away

My hands and feet

All numb

When I sneeze and cough

Will they be signs

Of what is yet

To come?

When I can not

Sing or dance

Outside

Will I be cast?

A year, a month

A day or two

How long will

My life last?

Contemplation

I wish I were a raft
Thrown out
Into the sea
Or a rope tied around
The bark of a tree

I wish I were a whistle
Blowing at
Flashing lights
Or a warm pair
Of gloves
To fight a frost
That bites

I wish I were a cork
In the barrel

Of a gun
Or a solid, wooden block
When all the cutting's done

I wish I were a bottle
With a cap
To turn
Or a morning shower
To cool the flames
That burn

I wish I were a cup
Of water, coffee, tea
I just wish I were able
To save myself
From me

The Quest

Up all night
Eyes full of tears
Trickling down
For endless years
In the dark
Remiss of day
Love and hope
Both cast away
Feeling weak
And soul, so sad
To miss a life
I never had
Like a dream
Almost unreal

With a longing

To reveal

A brighter day

A quest to see

The light of day

And hope for me

On the brink of

My explode

And the truth

I shall behold

Rays that will

Forever shine

To ease my weak,

Troubled mind

And heal my aching,

Bleeding heart

Comfort, someday,

Will impart

A peaceful path

My earnest plea

To the haven

I shall see

Change

Like a rainy day in May
Becomes a sunny June
From the waking of the sun
To the slumber of the moon

The thorny budding rose
Is, too, a soft gift of love
From a creature of the Earth
To its flutter up above

The crying newborn babe
Will have a song to sing
His noises in the night
Will surely someday ring

Like the shine of something new
Will see tarnish when it's old
From a weak and wailing lad to
A fighter, fierce and bold

Like it's wrestle with the wind
Becomes the humming of a bird
From a fearless soldier
To a wand'ring soul unheard

To bear the heat of the sun
Then shower of the rain
Once ready to run a race, then
Body be wrecked with pain

Like feeling fancy free
To facing an unknown
From laughing with a friend
To crying all alone

Like wishing a day could last
But knowing it, too, will end
From a lonely, broken heart
To one true love can mend

Like winter becomes spring
And summer greets the fall
From the opening song
To a last and final call

Everything

In life must change.

First Love

Oh how I love the
King of Kings
Who reigns o'er my life
The Almighty Healer
Of my misery and strife
Oh how I love the
Precious Lamb
So innocent, so pure
I call him The Great I Am
That always has a cure
Oh how I love the
Lord of Lords
Ruler of mankind
Omnipotent Shepherd with
Lost sheep, he aims to find

Oh how I love the Prince of Peace

His grace and his love

And bless him for the many gifts

He showers from above

For the sick, the hungry,

And the ailing soul

He's the Balm in Gilead

His love will make you whole

Oh how I love the Rock

In a weary land

If I should falter, if I fall

He's there to hold my hand

Oh how I love my Savior

The forgiver of my sins

He will, someday, call me home

And, lovingly, let me in

Oh how I love the Holy One

That marched from hall to hall

For a wretch undone,
My Rose of Sharon did it all
Oh how I love My Everything
For dying on Calvary
Oh how I love Sweet Jesus
Because he first loved me

Great God

When there's no food on my table
And I'm down to my last dime
I remember, God is able
Always right on time
My God is everywhere
At all times, in every place
When I need him, he's right there
I just thank him for his grace
When I am weak, have fallen down
He's there to pick me up
When I was lost, 'twas me he found
With love, he filled my cup
On every dark and dreary day
He hears my ev'ry moan

A comfort as I kneel and pray

I know I'm not alone

My Father, Oh how great is he,

His spirit, and his love

My struggles, he can clearly see

With his loving eyes above

My Everything, he's so sweet

He's righteous, holy, true

My God's giving, can't be beat

His will, I must do

Where he will lead me, I don't know

Until sent, I'll stand still

When he sends me, I must go

For his arms, I long to feel

On mountain tops and valleys, low

I will honor him with praise

He's God on land, across the sea

Great in many ways

Many blessings he will pour

And will do just what he said

When closed, he opens each door

From darkness, me, he led

Until I'm called and hear my name

Servant—Come enter the gate

I won't sing for fortune or shout for fame

But worship him as I wait

A gracious God who has blessed in the past

Will bless over and again

His mercy and love will forever last

Great God!

      Hallelujah!

         Amen

Perfect Gifts

To you
I give the birds
That soar throughout the sky

To you
I give the land
Valley low and mountain high

To you
I give the waters
Each ocean, lake and sea

To you
I give the air
So plentiful and free

To you
I give the trees
Full of life, standing tall

To you
I give the seasons
Winter, Spring, Summer, Fall

To you
I give the sun
That brightens up each day

To you
I give the laughter
Of a child at play

To you
I give the stars
That twinkle in the night

To you

I give the moon

With it's soft, radiant light

To you

I give my love

For the many things you do

To you

I give these gifts

Perfect gifts, I give to you

Ode to the Butterfly

Where are you?
Most cherished creature of grace
Clothed in nature's finest skin
We long to see your face
The daffodils await your flight
and flutter in the air
We all reach out to feel
The colorful coat you wear
The grass and sea await
Your debut across the sky
Patiently, silently
Oh sweet butterfly

Beauty is your backdrop
The sea and jet black sand

The flowery beds are your stage

On which you soon will stand

We welcome your descent

Our rainbow, like rays, shine

So pure, so lovely, innocent

So one of a kind

For you, the birds do sing

And trees, they bow down

A gracious heavenly body,

In you, the world has found

Portrait of Home

acres of green

and oceans of blue

streets of gold

and rose petals too

milk and honey

streaming down

to each beat

and trumpet sound

a star, so bright

it shines above

an air of peace,

of mercy, of love

so wild, so free

the birds that fly

soaring, free-wheeling

up in the sky

with glory so tall

and goodness so wide

they unite with beauty

on every side

rivers touched

by each simple breeze

ripple softly

so calm, at ease

precious wonders

they, too, are found

oh the awesomeness

around

showers of blessings,

manifold

that fills the heart

and frees the soul

a special place where
all time stands still
and love, true love
all creatures feel
acres of green
and oceans of blue
streets of gold
and rose petals too

Someday we'll be together.

About the Author

John Dwayne Evans, affectionately known as Jondee, was born and raised in the housing projects of Chicago's west side on April 3rd, 1974. With the loving support of his Mother, Patricia Evans, two sisters, Rita and Patricia (Jewel), teachers and administrators, and church family members, he spent much time writing and competing successfully in talent competitions.

In 1988, John graduated John M. Smyth Elementary School as class valedictorian. For the next four years, John was enrolled in Chicago's largest public high school, Lane Tech, where he studied Engineering and Science. He was active in the school's Black Student Union, Drama Club and Gospel Choir. In the summer of 1992, John won first place in the local NAACP ACT-SO (Academic, Cultural, Technical, Scientific Olympics) competition and second place in the national competition held in Nashville, Tennessee.

John graduated Lane Technical High School in the year 1992 and pursued higher education. Without an idea of how he would pay his tuition, John boarded a Greyhound bus bound for Atlanta, Georgia and visited Morris Brown College. After auditioning with the concert choir directors, Glenn Halsey and Ruth Stokes, he received a partial choir scholarship. John's college career was underway.

During John's four-year tenure at Morris Brown College, he participated in a variety of extracurricular activities and received numerous academic scholarships. Some of the organizations included: Phi Mu Alpha Sinfonia (Professional Music) Fraternity of America, Marketing Club, New Black Voices Drama Guild, Concert and Gospel Choirs, and Student Council. John submitted several articles and poems to the school newspaper and creative writing magazine.

John graduated Morris Brown College with Cum Laude honors in the spring of 1996 and earned a Bachelor of Science degree in Marketing. Upon graduation, he worked as Business Analyst, Operations Specialist, and Operations Reporter for Electronic Data Systems (EDS) in Detroit, Michigan. "Acres of Green and Oceans of Blue: Diary of a Runaway," John's first collection of original poetry, takes the reader on one man's journey as he searches within himself and goes on a quest for love and respect. John's greatest ambition is to encourage the reader to love self, life and fellow man. John currently resides in Chicago, Illinois where he continues to write, sing and teach.

0-595-01033-4